"I do not know how he does it, but Julio's nonsense totally makes sense."
—Isabella Rossellini

THE Perfect Gift

Julio Torres

SIMON & SCHUSTER
New York Amsterdam/Antwerp London
Toronto Sydney/Melbourne New Delhi

Simon & Schuster
1230 Avenue of the Americas
New York, NY 10020

First Simon & Schuster hardcover edition November 2026

SIMON & SCHUSTER and colophon are registered trademarks of Simon & Schuster, LLC

Photographer: Joe Caster
Interior designer: William Ruoto
Illustrator: Max Wittert
Graphic designer: Mateo Garcia
Photo shoot producer: May Kielany
Makeup: Cyler D'aigle
Styling: Angel Emmanuel
Set decorator: Will Casey

Manufactured in China

1 3 5 7 9 10 8 6 4 2

Library of Congress Control Number has been applied for.

ISBN 978-1-6680-0235-3
ISBN 978-1-6680-0237-7 (ebook)

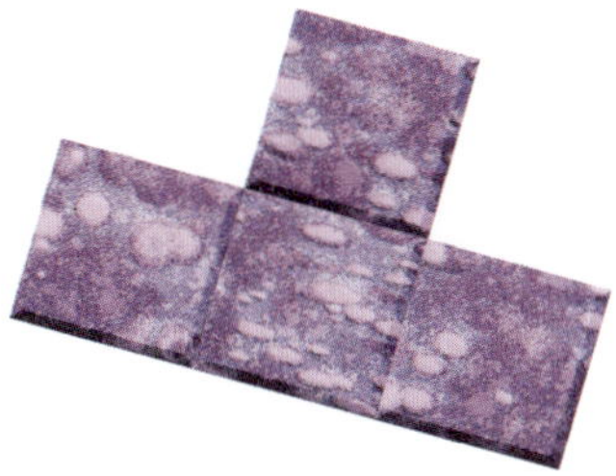

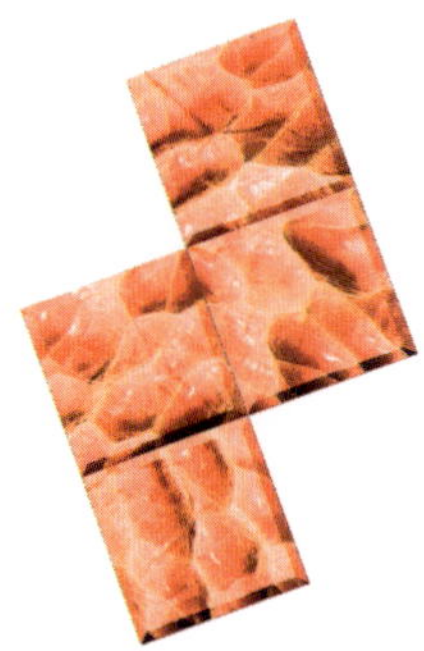

Introduction

Why do we give gifts? This question is not very relevant to me, because frankly the answers range from "to show love" to "because it was rude not to." If you're giving a gift, you know why you're doing it. Next question.

What makes a good gift? Now *this* is why you're holding this book. Many people think a lot about the person receiving the gift and ask themselves questions like "What do they like?" and "What do they need?" But I think that's just half of it. The real question is, What do you want your relationship with this other person to be?

Gifts aren't one directional. They're bridges. A good gift reflects the level of intimacy you have, or aspire to have, with the person receiving it.

Take the gift of fire, for example. Yes, fire. Prometheus gave humans fire, and we've certainly used it *a lot*. I just used it this morning to make oatmeal. It's very useful. But that's an assessment of fire, not of fire as a gift.

As a gift, fire is pretty loaded. A little condescending, if you think about it. Now, we owe this Prometheus person so much. Plus, given that he stole it, the gift came with lots of drama no one asked for. But hey, we do use it every day, so thanks, I guess.

What was Prometheus trying to say with this gift? What did he want the gift to do to our relationship? He wanted to be important to us. He understood that one of the ways someone becomes relevant in our lives is by helping us solve a tangible problem. In this case, there's the fact that without fire, birthday candles would just be little sticks. Plus, of course it allows us to see at night and to cook, etc. This achievement—becoming important to the receiver of the gift—is the high so many chase when they bestow a useful little gadget.

For example, I kept losing my passport, so someone I work with gifted me a passport case with an AirTag. It's been extremely helpful, and now I can't help but think of her every time I sigh in relief when I find my passport after briefly misplacing it. The gift works as intended, not just because I no longer lose my passport but because now I think, "Wow, Molly is very smart. I should keep giving her publicity firm thousands of dollars a month." She became Prometheus. That is what she wanted to do, and she succeeded. She thought about her relationship with me and how solving a tangible problem in my life would make up for the fact that we don't really have much in common.

Had she thought of just me rather than us, she would have given me a fun little trinket that would have gone into the room of fun little trinkets people give me (no shade; please keep them coming. I must have more).

Other gifts give us insight into how someone thinks of us. Name Drop Alert: Tilda Swinton once gave me a pendant of a yellow ceramic balloon. She chose a symbol. What did she say with this gift? It's certainly not something I "needed" or something I had been eyeing in any way, but it's a window into how my friend thinks of me. A yellow balloon is whimsical, joyful, playful—the fact that it reminded her of me makes me very happy. It gave me insight into how she feels about our friendship, and thus made me feel closer to her.

My friend David gifted me a little red spiral mobile he found in his parents' attic. I love it. It made me realize he thinks of me even when I'm not in front of him, which by "gay guy in New York" standards is pretty meaningful. The red mobile is also a piece of his home, but a piece that didn't quite fit in, hence why it was forgotten in the attic. Him giving that to me, like Tilda's yellow balloon, helps me understand our dynamic from his point of view. He's saying, "You appreciate odd things that come from my home." Perhaps he's also saying, "You understand *me*." Sure, maybe it's just about the spiral mobile being kind of odd "like my friend Julio," but I think we're both the spiral. Maybe Tilda feels like a yellow balloon when she works with me. Aw, I hope that's true.

Neither the spiral nor the balloon were given to me for any particular occasion. I enjoy gifts that are like hugs—gifts that are a warm, casual embrace among those you love. In fact, I don't think I've ever given a gift to someone I didn't like or am even ambivalent about. I don't give gifts out of duty, but rather when something calls to me and reminds me I want to "hug" a friend.

I do understand, however, that a lot of you holding this book do occasionally "have to" give gifts, and often you don't even have enough insight into a person to help them with a problem (like the passport holder), nor do you even want to build on the relationship in any way. Not every gift has to be a heart-to-heart.

For example, nothing says "whatever" more than giving a woman a candle. It's a gesture that says, "There, I did it." But maybe that's what you're going for. Sometimes you just have to pay a little toll, by giving a man a tie or an in-law a bottle of wine. These gifts are like walls, guarding us from each other. They're the equivalent to "How are you doing?" "Fine." There, you're done with that interaction—now you can move on. At this level of intimacy, you only need a very superficial knowledge of the person receiving the gift in order to find one for them. Heck, sometimes you only need to know their gender (flowers = lady; scotch = man). This book won't dwell much on those kinds of gifts, so in the spirit of "getting it over with," let's continue.

Section One

Gifts That Are Like Fire

Like the legend of Molly the Publicist giving me the passport holder with the AirTag, gifts like Prometheus's fire to mankind are useful, sometimes even life-changing, and cement the gift giver as indispensable.

For this kind of gift, it is *crucial* to have a solid understanding of the specificity of the receiver's life. This means you must think of the person first—don't start with the gift. Many people make the mistake "around the holidays" of buying useful little gadgets for people without asking themselves, "Is this gift useful to this person *specifically*?" I have received many presents that the givers thought were intended to be like fire, but weren't. One time I got some kind of thing I can't even name, which I guess is to rest a mixing spoon (?) on while cooking. Like, what? I don't cook. I don't even have the tool that this subtool is supposed to help with. No one wants a solution for a problem they don't have.

Imagine if Prometheus had given fire to moles, who can live their lives perfectly without light. Or to fireflies? Or deep-sea fish? They'd be like, "Okay . . ."

If there's no problem, there's no reason for a solution. If you give someone something they do not need, you are giving them a problem. It's like an unwanted house call.

If executed correctly, these gifts should feel like, say, a fence between friendly neighbors. You get to chat about something not too intimate ("Thank God it's finally summer!" not "I might leave my husband").

TODD SNYDER

Olympic Torch

This is for a young, metropolitan person who cares about their relatives on a theoretical level but doesn't want to spend much time with them.

Every now and then, we must pay one of the taxes of living in "polite society": A relative comes to visit, and they want to get brunch. Near the end of the meal, they may suggest going on a walk or having you join them on a trip to a flea market, or they could make another little request that might prolong your time together ("My daughter saw a famous cupcake store online, where is it? I want to send her a picture"). If that happens, simply take out this replica of the Olympic Torch and say, "Oh shoot, I'd love to keep this going, but I was in the middle of handing this over! The torch simply must remain on its journey so it can make the ceremony in time. But let me know when you're back in town, okay?"

Warning: flammable.

The Darkness Eater

A vial that sucks in darkness, immediately brightening up the room. It's better than a flashlight or a lamp because those products simply mask darkness with artificial light that is harmful to our senses (mostly hearing; trust me). They're the light equivalent of concealing odors with Febreze rather than actually getting rid of the smell. But the Darkness Eater traps darkness, restoring the original bright room that was under it, costing only about an hour of your total lifespan per cubic centimeter you undarken.

This gift is for someone who is fussy about lighting and is also the kind of person who cares about the ingredients in household products (e.g., aluminum in deodorant, etc.).

Giuseppino, the Tip Elf

This is the ideal gift for your boss, uncle, or older person in your life who doesn't trust themselves to use technology to fix a problem and is soothed by a middleman. The kind of person who uses an accountant instead of self-filing their taxes through a website; the kind of person who uses a travel agent.

Calculating the tip is very difficult. Especially with the pressure of being at a restaurant, with everyone looking at you, or worse, waiting for you to give up the table. Maybe you know what percentage you want to leave, but good *luck* figuring out how much money that is.

That's where Giuseppino comes in. He provides the service of calculating the tip for you, so you can enjoy your meal knowing there's no stress when the check comes. Giuseppino is an elf, about four inches tall, who you'd hire on a full-time basis, regardless of how often you need your tip calculated. To summon his services, you must gently wake him up from the nap he's taking in your shirt pocket* and place him on the check. Then allow some time for him to stretch and get settled on the math problem. Giuseppino will then, using his abacus, determine the tip after he has conducted a brief interview with you about the service. If your answers feel biased, he may want to conduct a secondary interview with the server to determine the fairness of your answers. Remember: even though you are responsible for hiring Giuseppino, he is at the service of The Tip, not you. Think of him as an unbiased third-party consultant who sleeps in your pocket.

Should the total of the bill be a Difficult Number, like one ending in an odd number of cents, Giuseppino will raise his Difficult Number Flag, thus determining that the problem is too complicated for his abacus. (There are no half balls on his abacus, so how is he to deal with decimals?) He will then ask you to help out using the calculator app on your smartphone.

Giuseppino takes 30 percent of the total bill for each tip he helps calculate.

You may be wondering, "What about restaurants that have the portable tap-to-pay thingies that calculate the tip for you?" Please do not mention these to him, and act as if they're not there. And *please* do *not* ask him to help you split the bill with your friends. He is a Tip Elf, not a Split Elf. He did not go to school for that, nor does he have any respect for that lesser trade.

---

* Yes, you ***must*** wear a shirt with a pocket he can nap in, like in a hammock of sorts, and ***yes*** you must use hushed tones when he's sleeping, which is most of the day.

THANK YOU!
Side of rice........................ $7.99
Add chives $1.25
Shredded beef bowl $26.70
Arepas black bean $15.49
Arepas cheese $18.49
"Can I get the bowl but from the place across the street?"...................... $42.99
Nine dollars and ninety-nine cents in quarters...................... $9.99
Changing tables 3 times over perceived draft.............. $27.99
Sub total.......................... $150.89
Sales tax $5.29
Total $156.18
TIP:
TOTAL:

Ledge Seat

You probably haven't noticed these impediments to sitting unless you're killing time in Midtown Manhattan and want to briefly sit on a ledge. I'm talking about the metal spikes placed all over the city preventing people, particularly unhoused people, from resting on ledges, low walls, or any flat surface that could provide a brief respite from walking around. Fuck those spikes.

Here's a gift for the community: the Ledge Seat. It's a portable thick foam seat anyone can place over the spikes and sit comfortably without feeling them. It even comes with a cupholder and fan for ultimate comfort. Buy it and leave it over any of these spikes, anywhere in the city, and let it welcome a tired traveler. As a bonus, the sides have almost invisible prickly scales (like the skin of a shark) to prevent cops and landlords from removing them. A taste of their own medicine, if you will.

This is the perfect gift for someone you've never met.

CLOSED
FOR
RENOVATIONS

Closed for Renovations

Is your friend getting a hair transplant? Okay then, is he aware his scalp will be red and kind of hard to look at for a while? He can wear this curtain to hide his forehead. It's a great way to say, "Excuse our appearance while we renovate!"

Tiny Little Stairs

This is the perfect gift for that friend who has terrible sleep. Nightmares, insomnia, waking up tired and lethargic—these are all symptoms of restless dreams. Tiny Little Stairs are a solution for that: place these stairs, which are about three centimeters in height, next to your ear at night so your dreams can come out and dance.

You see, dreams get restless inside your head. If they can't come out and have a little fun, they get all fussy and cranky—these are called nightmares. Tiny Little Stairs allows them to descend from your ear and dance on your pillow. Once they've had their fun, they can return through the ear in a calm and stable fashion.

How else are dreams supposed to get down to your pillow, if not via Tiny Little Stairs?

Tiny Little Stairs are available in a few variations:

- The classic grand staircase, for those waltzing dreams that want to make an entrance
- A simple, clean staircase, for those no-fuss dreams
- And an escalator, for those dreams that are a little lazy

All Tiny Little Stairs come with handrails, because some of your dreams are old.

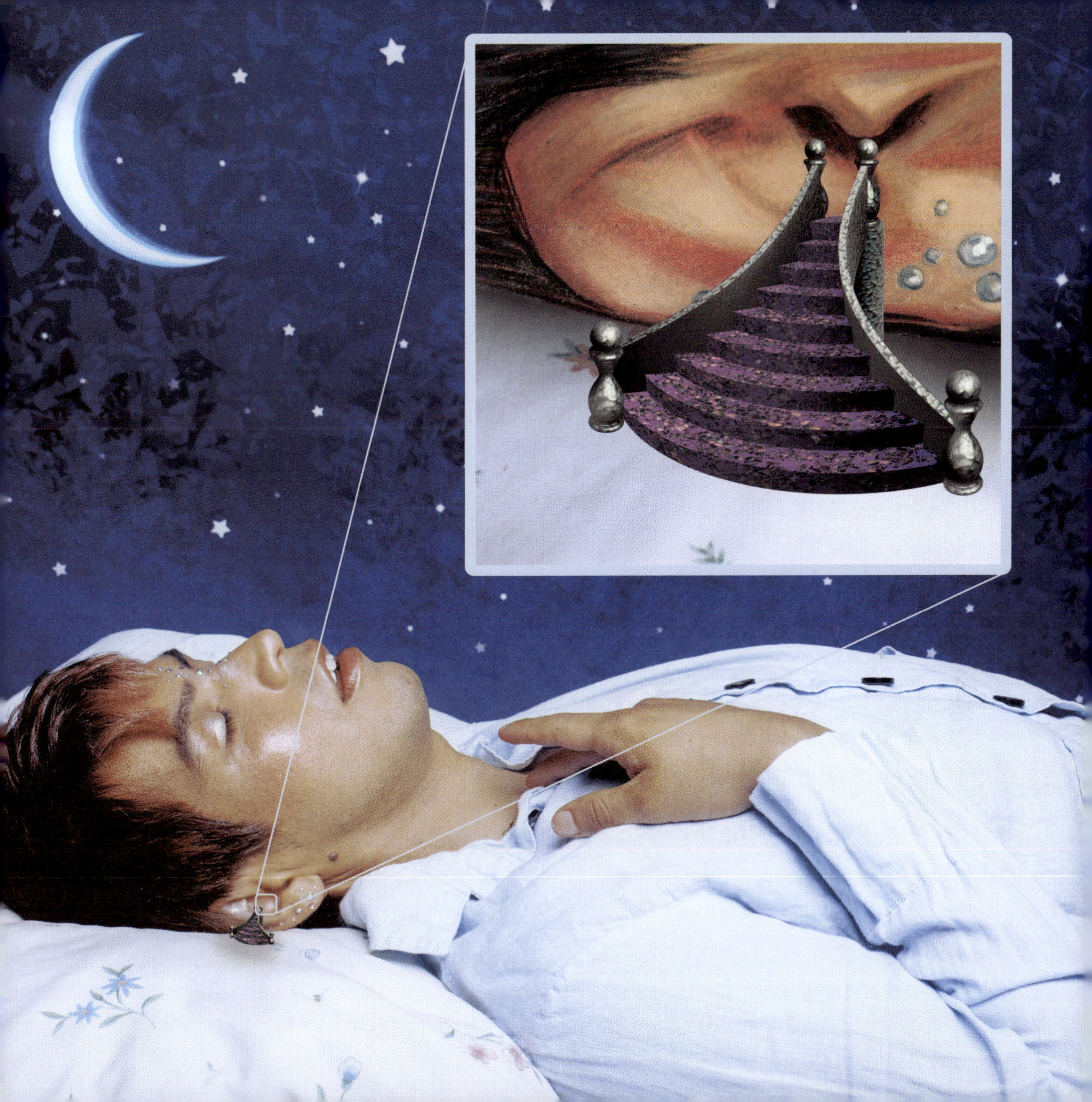

A Good Printer

A printer that works, and works all the time.

Who is this for: most of the world population.

Safe Music Box

A music box that can only be locked from the inside, by the ballerina. Who is this for? Well, the ballerina, of course.

Cords-Be-Gone

One time I answered a job ad placed by a woman named Vivian who was disturbed by the cords on her lamps. “They truly ruin a gorgeous object. Cords are so vulgar. I understand that’s how they gulp up electricity, but I don’t need to see how the sausage is made.”

She went on to compare seeing lamps plugged in to seeing someone “go number two.”

I suggested a battery pack, but she equated that to a diaper. After days of brainstorming with electricians, architects, and physicists, I found a suitable solution through a chemist who had devised a twice-daily pill to make the color fuchsia imperceptible to the patient.

And so, I painted every cord in her home fuchsia and instructed her staff to give her the pill two times a day, like the chemist recommended. The results were pretty quick, with minimal side effects (just an occasional rash between her fingers). Vivian finally saw no cords. "Thank you," she said to me while scratching her hands. "I really don't need to see how the sausage is made."

As I left her house, I felt slightly guilty that I didn't get rid of the cords like she had asked, but rather had tricked her into not seeing something upsetting to her. But why was it so upsetting to her? Why would someone choose a rash over investigating a phobia? Are solutions to small problems in some way merely a distraction from a bigger, deeper issue that keeps being swept under the rug? Well, she's happy for now. Plus she's just some lady who hired me, I told myself. I really don't need to know how the sausage is made.

Who is this gift for? Vivian, or someone eager to not see something that perhaps they should see.

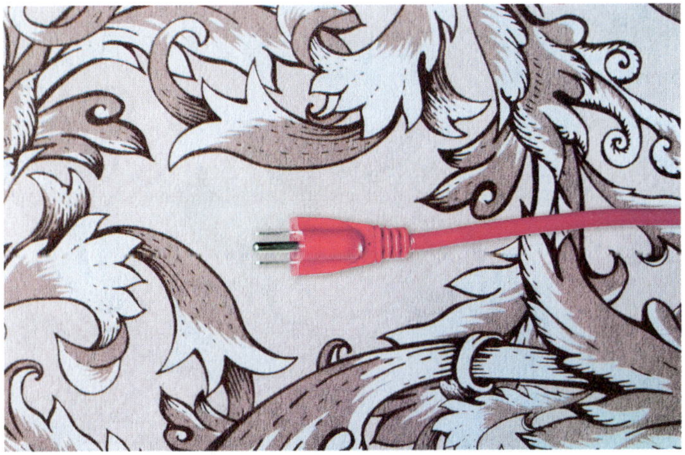
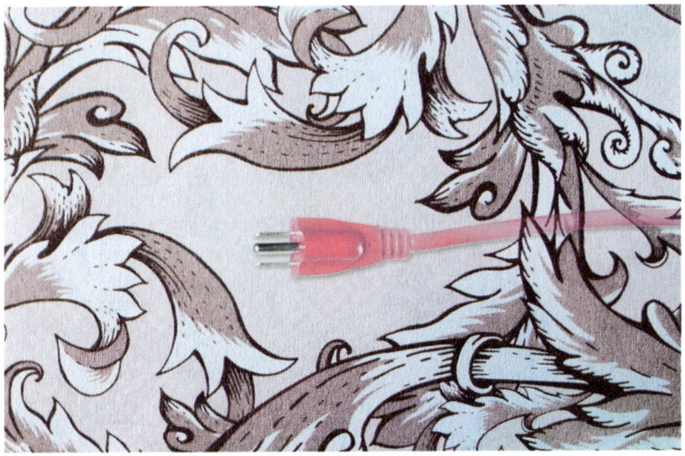

Razor X

A gift for that man in your life who insists on creating a jawline through shaving by arbitrarily deciding where their neck ends and their face begins. These types of men are, I suppose, envious of their peers with strong, obvious jawlines and want to do their best imitation of that by eyeballing where their beard "should" end. Most fail, resulting in a look that makes it seem as if their face is floating in a sea of body.

Razor X uses X-ray technology to determine where the jaw actually is by beeping loudly and repeating, "End beard here. End beard here."

You can't release a man from the prison of masculinity, but you can give him a fantastic shave.

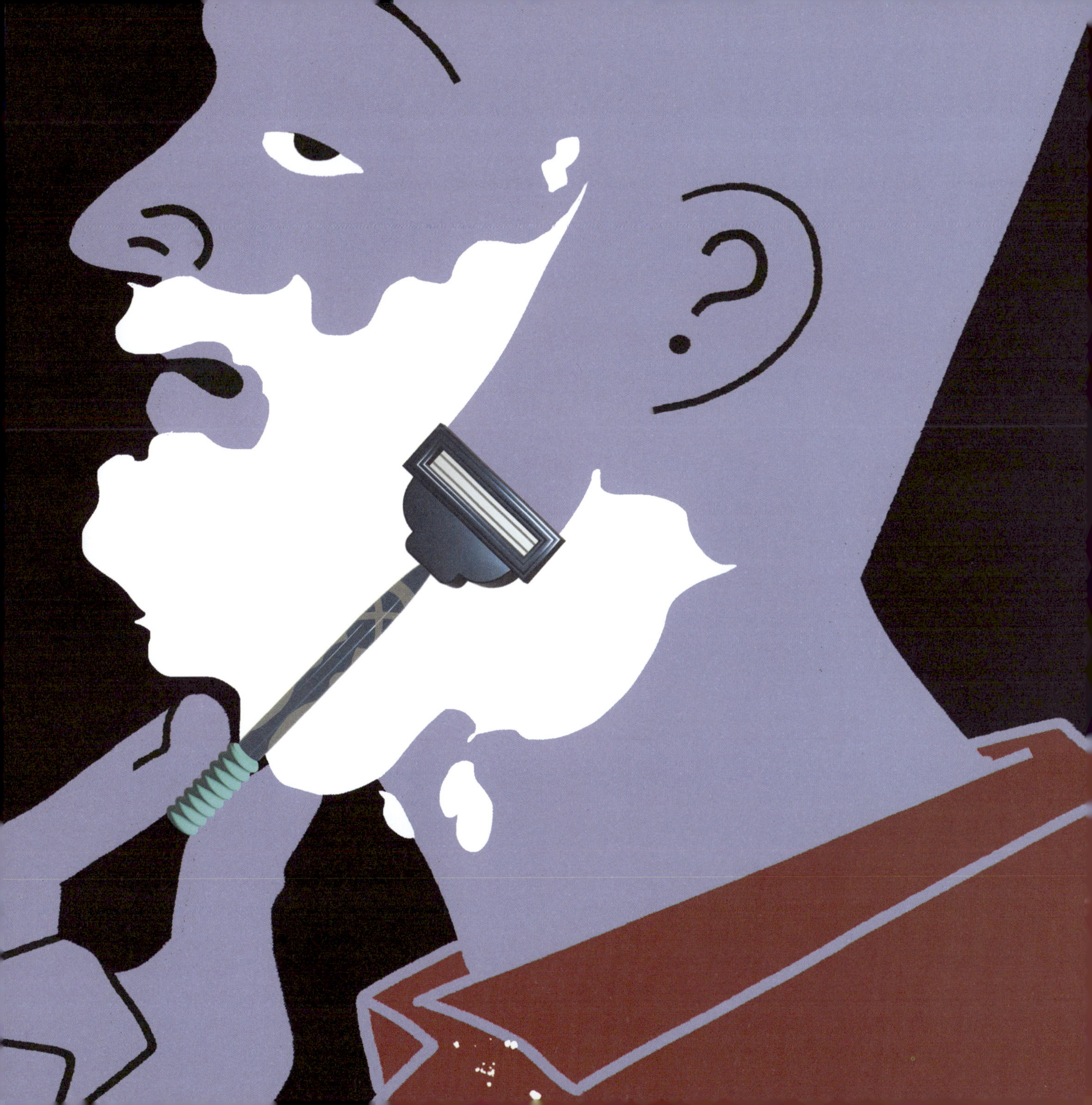

Umbrella for Men

A gift ideal for a heterosexual man who just can't get over himself.

Some men have an aversion to umbrellas. Something about them being "gay"? Gift them the Umbrella for Men. It's a regular umbrella, but it's branded in a "masculine" way that evokes strength, muscle cars, and fast-paced action sequences. An umbrella that doesn't say, "I'm a dainty little thing who can't handle a few raindrops," but says, "I am a MAN, and this is not an umbrella, this is my TOOL OF DEFENSE." I gave one to my friend's boyfriend Steven because I was sick of seeing him wet all the time. At least I think his name is Steven.

kravy
CHAZE

Ant Office

It's useless calling them "ant farms" given that urban ants, like us, have moved away from farming to the day-to-day grind of the office. And I'm not even talking cubicles; ants have moved on to open-floor offices. This kit starts the ants off in a modern office setting, where instead of collecting and storing food from the surface, office ants get together to think of better ways to entice the colony to *pay* for the food given by your hand.

The casualness and ease in their office infrastructure (couches, nectar on tap, standing desks) misguides the ants into believing their work conditions have gotten "better." But what we see in this microcosm is that even though they no longer farm, and no longer refer to their leader as "queen" but rather "CEO," upward mobility and wealth gaps have actually remained the same.

The ants spend the first chunk of their day performing niceties to each other (a ritual they were spared from back in their farming days) and the rest anxiously at their work stations, silently suffering under the tyranny of an open floor plan where they can be seen and heard by their superiors or, worse, each

other at all times. No office ant is safe from sudden layoffs, no matter what the "You Belong" mural in the hallways says.

Ants often have virtual meetings, begging the question "Why do we come to the office at all?" A question many are too scared to ask.

This gift is for anyone looking for a little meta-distraction at work. Take a break from the tedium of office life to stare at ants experiencing the tedium of office life.

security

Shadow Clothes

A gift for your shadow.

You see your shadow every day. Have you ever for a second stopped to think about its needs? Okay, well did you know that shadows are forced to wear the same clothes their Sources (their human counterparts) wear?

Shadow Clothes offer shadows the ability to express themselves by selecting what *they* want to wear. Just because they're replicating the Source's every movement doesn't mean they don't have opinions of their own!

One of These?

Not sure what it is.
Who is this for? You tell me.

Sublet Map

Many people sublet their apartments while they go on vacation, or sublet a room they don't use, to make ends meet.

Sure, in an ideal world, an adult who works a full-time job would be able to afford an apartment full-time. But don't think about that too much or you'll get radicalized (i.e., angry and sad all the time). Try the Sublet Map instead!

The Sublet Map is a system that allows you to maximize the space in your apartment. Allow the Sublet Scanner Bot to track your movements in your apartment for a week to come up with a document that details which parts of your apartment you currently use, and when. We guarantee you're not using *every* inch of it *all day*.

On this map, the Sublet Scanner Bot suggests alternative routes and times for you to use the space, allowing it to then create the most efficient and lucrative Sublet Map, which shows you which parts of your apartment to rent and when!

You could end up with up to twelve roommates in a two-bedroom apartment if you all stick to your designated times and spaces! It's kind of heartbreaking, though, to realize that if all the roommates weren't so invested in avoiding each other, in silencing the discomfort of having to share such a small space, and actually looked each other in the eyes and commiserated in their shared circumstance . . . a revolution could actually start.

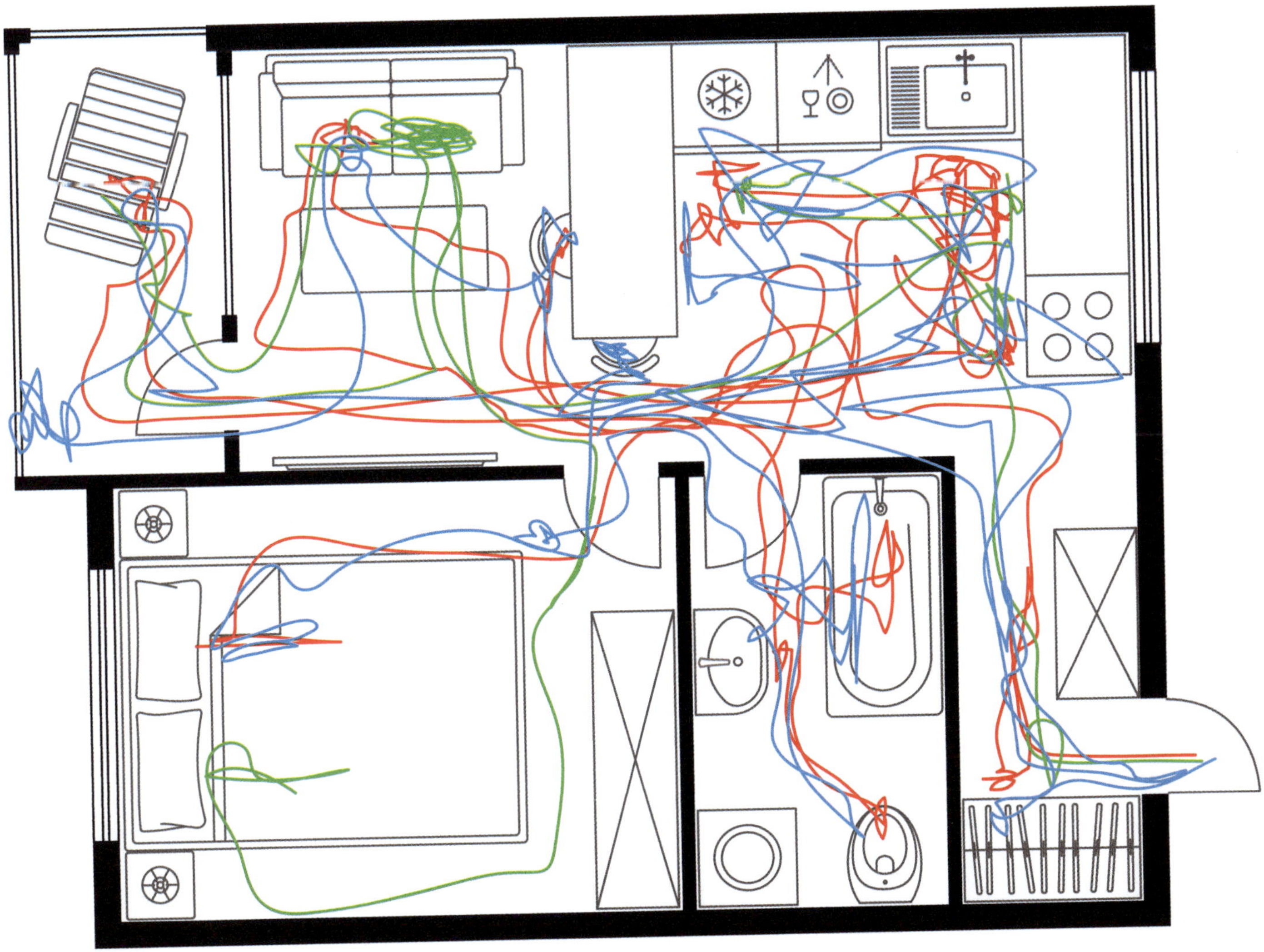

PERSON	COLOR
YOU	
SUB LETTER	
SUB LETTER 2* USES SAME SIDE OF BED BUT IS BARTENDER SO DOES NOT OVERLAP FOR SLEEP	

The CEO Flute

This is a gift for an entire city.

You have probably heard the tale of the Pied Piper of Hamelin, about a man who drove all the rats out of a town by luring them with the melody of his magical flute. Well, this flute does the same but with billionaires. What to most of us sounds like a few simple notes, billionaires will hear as the siren call of unlimited wealth, treasures far beyond anything they have already sucked out of the world. Sure, they might already have more money than they can spend in a lifetime or even generations, but this melody hypnotizes with the promise of more, more, more.

In Hamelin, the rats fell off a cliff—and listen, I'm trying to get this book published, so I will suggest no such thing—so instead, this flute lures billionaires into a facility that will treat the mental illness that is savage, uncontrollable greed. Through a combination of therapy and *A Christmas Carol*–esque visions, these Big Tech Scrooges will come back healthier and ready to admit that it would be okay to concede to a fair distribution model in which everyone's basic human needs are covered—leaving them, well, still obscenely rich.

Patient Grandson

There comes a time when every thirtysomething realizes we don't know how to work a piece of technology. Maybe we lost our contacts when buying a new phone, or maybe we can't get our Venmo balance into our bank account. When friends and lovers get impatient, it's time to hire Patient Grandson.

Patient Grandson will send a lovely kid of about eleven years old to come and sit with you as they not only solve your problem but show you how to solve it yourself! The kid will even nod respectfully as you mutter about how complicated the iPad is or that the company does it on purpose. No little tirade or tech oopsie is too burdensome for a Patient Grandson.

Roach Resort

Anyone will tell you it's very, very difficult to get rid of roaches for good. So why not send them to a resort? That way, you both catch a break!

The Roach Resort offers free shuttles to pick up the roaches from your home. A standard shuttle fits up to one hundred, and a megashuttle up to five hundred. Make sure you have a head count before booking, and please ensure the roaches show up on time, typically around 2:34 a.m.

The shuttle will take them to their accommodations, followed by all-you-can-eat buffets, optional massages, and unlimited pool time.

When friends come over and remark on how you got rid of the roaches, feel free to say, “They’re just away on vacation,” and give them our brochure.

This gift is as much for the roaches as it is for that roach-infested friend in your life.

Baby's First Insurance Nightmare

Many toys are designed to introduce children to an adult idea or habit. Kids can pretend to be doctors, chefs, race car drivers . . . but what are the chances they'll actually do any of that when they grow up? Shouldn't playing pretend train them for when life isn't just fun and games?

That's why there's Baby's First Insurance Nightmare! It comes with a pile of colorful plastic medical bills charging exorbitant amounts that far exceed the play money the babies are also given. The bills have buttons they must press in the right order, at the right time, to get to different parts of the game.

Baby's First Insurance Nightmare connects them with babies in other houses who are playing Baby's First Minimum Wage Job, and who are not particularly incentivized to help the sick baby. The game can go on for years! Also, for a more accurate Insurance Nightmare experience, the baby must play this game while wearing a plastic cast and using crutches.

Baby gifts, as you know, are usually for the parents' idea of who that baby should be. This is for young parents who want their baby to be prepared.

BILL

Baby's First Minimum Wage Job

For kids who are swarmed with calls from kids playing Baby's First Insurance Nightmare.

Crystal Network

Here's something for that someone in your life who keeps buying crystals but can't get them to "work." Perhaps it's not the crystals' fault they can't fix bad energy or back pain. Buying more is certainly not going to help with the money problems. What the crystals may need is access to the Crystal Network.

This subscription-based resource allows the crystals in any given home to access online forums with other crystals all over the world and share tips and tricks for helping their humans. Maybe a rose quartz can't cure writer's block, but before you go and buy something else, have the quartz check the Crystal Network for tips from a citrine.

The rose quartz simply needs to be placed in front of the crystal tablet, create a crystal account, and access the hundreds of forums dedicated to all kinds of human problems and ailments.

Crystals can also earn online associate's degrees in management, communications, and even fashion merchandising. That way, they're not just limited to "healing the aura" of your space but they can also book your flights, manage web purchase returns, and even reheat your leftovers.

Shattered Mirror

Not sure what to give that teenager going off to college? How about a Shattered Mirror for their dorm room, ideal for after their first wild night out of self-discovery, so when they come back the next morning having not done their homework, ignored calls from their parents, and burned god knows how many bridges with the friendships they built their first semester, they can look at themselves and ask, "What have I become?"

Clean Floor Jet Pack

Having a shoes-off policy is a great way of keeping your floors clean, but it can get a little annoying. This gift is perfect for that someone in your life who cares more about solutions than examining the root of the problem. Like my friend Simon, for example, who was constantly scolded by his partner, Rita, for walking on their floors with his shoes on.

Simon always took off his shoes when entering the apartment, so that wasn't the issue per se. It was that he'd get ready to leave, put on his shoes, and then realize he'd left his keys somewhere in the kitchen and rush back to get them without taking off his shoes again, for fear that would make him late. "I'm just popping back in quickly, what's the big deal?" he'd ask. To which Rita would reply, "Just because you're doing it quickly doesn't mean that your shoes are any less dirty." He tried tiptoeing back, but that didn't ease the tension. She put a bowl by the door for his keys, but he never used it. "I'm not doing it on purpose, I just forget," he'd argue. "What's the big deal?"

So I gave him the Clean Floor Jet Pack, which allowed him to hover over his floors rather than putting his shoes back on.

Unfortunately, the smell of gasoline, noise, and moderate-but-still-noticeable gusts of wind it created in the apartment made Rita even more upset.

She stayed in bed as he was getting ready to leave for the day. Typical Simon, when he already had his shoes on by the door, he realized he'd forgotten his wallet on the nightstand. So he strapped on the jet pack and swooshed over to the bedroom, waking Rita up, which was an upsetting first thing for her to deal with in the morning.

"We need to talk," she said as he was floating out of the room.

"I'm running late!" he shouted over the sound of the roaring engine.

"This isn't working out."

"What?"

"THIS ISN'T WORKING OUT!"

"I just don't have the time to do the whole shoe thing in the morning!"

"You are SO unwilling to think ahead, and meet me halfway, that you use a fucking spaceship that reeks of gasoline! It's wrecked the wallpaper, and it wakes me up, Simon!"

"I don't forget on purpose. What's the big deal?"

"You deciding not to change is purposeful. Can you come down from that fucking thing?"

"If I do, my shoes will touch the floor, and God forbid that happens. You'll be pissed at me all day again. It's like walking on eggshells with you."

"You're not walking on eggshells, Simon. You are incapable of doing the bare minimum, accuse me of being difficult for making a very simple request, and then attempt to solve it in a way that is soooo ridiculous, so dramatic, that it makes me out to be the crazy one! What do you tell people at work? 'I have to fly around the house because my bitch girlfriend is insane'?"

"No one's saying you're insane."

"I'm saying you are insane. Or manipulative, actually."

"Look, I don't have to use the Jet Pack, but my shoes will have to touch the floor."

"Incredible."

"What do you want me to do then?! I'm between a rock and a hard place here."

"You are the rock and you are the hard place."

"Are we still talking about the Jet Pack?"

"We never were."

Note: yikes!

Section Two

Gifts That Are Like the Statue of Liberty

France famously gave the United States the Statue of Liberty, and the United States really made it its own. This demonstrates a greater effort than gifting a solution like those in Section One, not because the damn thing had to be shipped in pieces, but because France had to know the United States pretty well in order to nail the gift.

France knew the United States was feeling itself as a whole "safe haven for immigrants," which, yes, was just a phase. Now the Statue of Liberty feels like a dinosaur poster in the room of a kid who is currently into spaceships but hasn't gotten around to changing the T-Rex poster. Regardless, this kind of gift doesn't just say, "I know what you like," but "I see who you want to be. I see you, and I want you to know that I see you."

Tilda's balloon and David's red spiral (from the intro; did you read that?) fall into this category. These gifts are about the bond between two people—not simply noting that it exists, but coloring the bond, shading it, giving it dimension. My friend Greta gave me a Schiaparelli brooch in the shape of an eye.

"I have two," she casually revealed. "I feel like you need one of them." With it, she says, "Yes, you see me as luxurious, but I see you as luxurious in your own way as well." My friend Spike gives me funny little toys he frequently finds on the sidewalk. To me, that says, "We found each other, we give each other meaning."

The Statue of Liberty gave the United States meaning, and deepened its relationship with France.

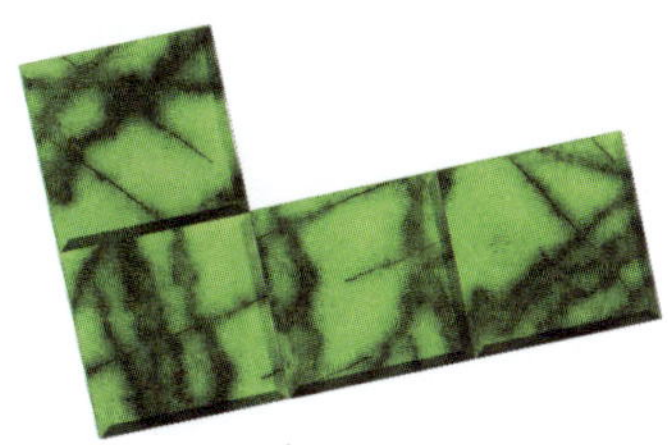

Sentient Silverware

Special-occasion silverware with a soul. Their screams of pain can be heard as they're chomped on, submerged in boiling soup, and concussed against champagne flutes when someone's making a toast. The perfect gift for someone in need of ruining a special occasion.

Perhaps they want to spoil an engagement, wreck a wedding shower, or scare away an investor. This gift says, “I know you have to host a fancy dinner, and I know you feel put upon by it—let this silverware scream for you.”

Walking Classes

My friend Ignacio lives by the beach and sees this one crab every day on his walk to work. They started hitting it off surprisingly well considering they're different species. Eventually, they got in the habit of going on morning walks together, which proved a little challenging given that the crab naturally walks sideways.

For the crab's birthday, my friend gave him a coupon for walking classes.

The crab took the coupon with his claw, brought it to his eyes, and went "?"

"Oh, well, they can teach you how to walk properly."

". . . ?"

"You know, teach you how to walk straight."

"—"

"It's just, well, I noticed on our walks that you walk sideways, which kinda makes it hard to walk with you. Like, it would be easier if you walked straight . . ."

". . ."

The crab placed the coupon on the ground and walked away sideways and offended.

What made Ignacio think the crab wanted to "correct" his walk? When giving a gift, it's important to ask whether it's for yourself or the person receiving it.

Apology Card

Ignacio went back to the crab the following day and handed him a card that simply read, "I'm sorry." The crab nodded, and from that day on they took turns: one day they'd walk straight; the other they'd walk sideways.

Menu

Spy Kit

Research shows some human couples out there are monogamous, kind of like penguins. This is perfectly natural, though it does leave room for "cheating"—a violation of the agreed-upon monogamy—where one partner has a secret affair with someone else (which, again, is *not* okay according to this practice).

If you have a friend with this lifestyle, they probably wonder from time to time if their partner is cheating on them. For them, there's this Spy Kit, which includes a scarf, sunglasses, a wig, and a tall menu to hide behind while the potentially unfaithful lover has a "lunch meeting" with his "business partner."

You wouldn't be providing the gift of a revelation. You'd be providing the gift of a thrill. The rush of jealousy and excitement that is ignited by suspicion is a pillar of the monogamous lifestyle.

Aquarian Tetris

The Aquarius brain cannot simply put a piece where it "fits." An Aquarius must feel out the needs of the piece and intuit where they want it to be. *Aquarian Tetris* is like regular *Tetris*, except pieces can fall wherever they want, and the game is completed

once it

“feels” right.

Résumé
Co. (2020 - 2025)
and media relations. Key
on relaunch of Pepsi App.
(2020 - 2020)

Résumé Pillow

It is some people's instinct to grab a couch pillow and cover their midsection when they sit down. It's both subconscious and self-conscious. This person has a deeply ingrained shame of their midsection caused by the fact that our society values thinness. Well, you can't really fix that with a gift, but you *can* help them lead with assets that actually matter.

The Résumé Pillow is customizable—you can have your friend's many achievements itemized and embroidered on it. You can even embroider their references in case the person sitting across from them really wants to double-check their GPA before judging them.

The next time your friend reaches for a pillow to hide themselves, they can also *show* others what they're proud of, even if it's just an embroidered screenshot of a tweet that went sort of viral.

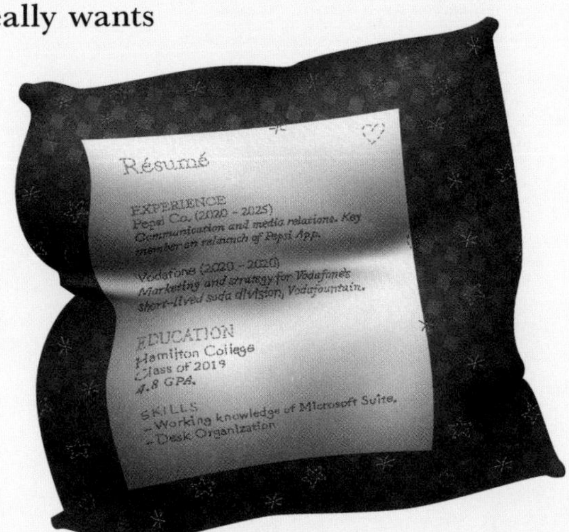

At
Capacity

At Capacity

People can be dismissive of strangers at parties not because they intend to, but simply because they're At Capacity. That means someone only has the emotional room for the people they came to the party with, or the people they already know, and doesn't have the energy to do the heavy lifting of getting to know someone new. There's no vacancy.

This hat has a neon sign that announces when someone is At Capacity, informing strangers to keep moving along.

Who is this for? That friend who simply cannot do it tonight, or any night. The friend who needs a respite from small talk; the friend that needs to hear, "It's okay to not want to talk to people all the time. I love you regardless and want to shield you from it."

BadMailMan.com

Hey, everyone has a kink, and this is an online subscription for those whose kink is to see a mailman go into a public restroom and read other people's letters.

Every titillating video starts with the mailman walking down the street, waving to the people in the neighborhood like there's nothing off about him. But then he gets to a public restroom. He brings in the mail, goes into a stall . . . and opens it. Carefully, of course. He's done this before. He reads every bank statement and every wedding invitation, and savors every item in a contractor's bill. He then puts the letters back together like nothing happened . . . No one will suspect. It's his little secret.

Gift this to a friend as a way of saying, "Yup, I know you more than you think. I won't tell a soul."

EAL LOVE
is this real love? is that what you even want?
THIS SICK AN
TWISTED BASTA
IS HAVING
MEDIOCRE SE
WITH HIS WIF
AND SHE STIL
LOVES HIM
CLICK TO FIN
OUT HOW
WHAT IS HI
SECRET????
2 INCHES I
IT'S BETTER TO JERK OFF WITH A FRIEND.
MAIL MAN
LION VIEWS | 12 MINUTES AGO
LO
HATE
SHARE
REPORT

Desktop Well

If your friend has a desk job, chances are it's, well . . . awful. They probably ache for time to ponder and reflect. A place to wish upon. A place to look at their reflection and wonder, "Is there a life away from this place?"

For them, there's the Desktop Well. A desktop Zen garden provides serenity, but a Desktop Well isn't to relieve stress. It's for something bigger. It's for melancholy. Melancholy for a life not yet lived. For adventure. For unfulfilled wishes.

The Desktop Well is made out of a handsome metal so as not to seem like a trinket but a stately tool on an executive's desk. An executive who needs to look at his reflection and sigh between pointless Zoom calls. He can tap on the water, look at the ripples, and ponder, "Does Big Oil love me back?" "Do adventures await beyond the walls of General Mills?" Perhaps. But not today. Today, your friend looks at charts. But for a moment, in the shallow waters of their Desktop Well, they see life.

DELETE FILE
Are you sure you want to burn this?
This file will be deleted forever

Safe Fire Logs

When you delete a file from your computer, or a picture from your phone, the software makes sure you stand by that decision by asking you a couple of times if you're sure and warning you that permanently deleting something cannot be undone.

But what if you're, say, burning an old lover's letters? Or tossing incriminating evidence from your corrupt husband into the fireplace, like he instructed you to do from jail? You might want to hold on to that as a bargaining chip during the divorce.

Safe Fire Logs produce fire capable of asking if you're sure about what you're about to do and not burning what you've tossed until you say, "I understand this cannot be undone."

This is for that person in your life who needs guardrails, who is impulsive and regrets it, and who needs an eraser as much as they need a pencil.

TindrINFINITY

An online dating subscription for gay guys who don't want to date people in open relationships, so it connects them with single goblins and demons from other dimensions, given that everyone here is taken.

XPLORE LIKES CHATS

hese creatures found you cute, message them to match!

L0veMast3r

SUPER LIKED ● ONLINE

"Hewwooooo kitten...daddy's hungwy tonight...and you s
the pwefect snack. UWU XOXO"

MATCH IGNORE

LOCATION: 4 mi
HEIGHT: 4'3
INTERESTS: Discord, Anime, Demonic Rituals

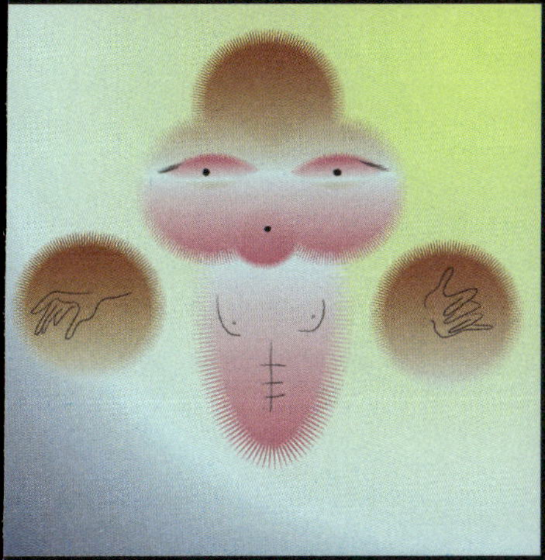

hello

○ LAST SEEN 5H AGO

"i want to touch you"

MATCH IGNORE

LOCATION: 0.5 mi
HEIGHT: 6'7
INTERESTS: Tarot, Breaking Bad, Astral Projection

ScarryJerry

● ONLINE

"AAAAAAAAAAAAAAAHHHHHHHHHHHHHHHHHHHHHHHHHHHHHHHHHHHH

MATCH IGNORE

LOCATION: Behind you
HEIGHT: 9'2

Betrenox

A gift for that friend who sees the glass as half empty. For the pessimist who doesn't live life because they're weighed down by all the what-ifs. "What if I go out and wake up late for my meeting?" "What if I do go to Brazil and get malaria?" "What if I fall in love and get my heart broken?"

Betrenox is a demon who eats fear. He comes in an egg that must be placed under the bed of the person who needs to be freed from their fears. As soon as an intrusive, negative thought manifests, Betrenox hatches, opens his mouth, and swallows the fear (which to him looks like a delicious gray cloud). The fear is now gone!

Betrenox will make a home for himself under the bed and be ready to devour any fear that may manifest, allowing your friend to travel, date—live life! The only drawback is that, if not fed, Betrenox may occasionally scream, "Feed me fear!" in the middle of the night or, if he's living under a particularly anxious person, balloon to the size of a pit bull.

Betrenox must go on a little walk every night. He won't do the walking, though; he must remain in his stroller as his human takes a lap around the block. Passersby may come up to the stroller thinking they'll see a cute baby or toy dog, but they'll know that's not what this is when they see his little claw peek from behind the stroller's veil, eager to yank fear out of the unsuspecting passerby to stuff his mouth with it.

Betrenox will live up to 130 years. He will outlive his human. He must then be walked by the human's next of kin. My friend Alex was too scared to ask a girl out until I got him Betrenox, who ate every anxiety that would have prevented him from going on a date, leaning in for a kiss, proposing, and now . . . having their first kid.

His son will have to push Betrenox in his stroller once Alex is long dead. He'll do it knowing he's pushing the weight of his father's fears, inside the belly of a demon who made it possible for him to even be alive.

Black Hole

Vivian called me again. This time she was distressed by the edge of the trash bag poking out from over the rim of her garbage can. "It's like seeing someone's underwear," she said. "I understand the trash bin needs a bag, but I just don't want to see how the sausage is made."

I mean, the woman did have a point. Even many of the slick, expensive trash cans have the plastic bag sticking out, which cheapens the object. I don't know that I have ever lost sleep over it like Vivan did (she hadn't slept in four weeks, apparently), but yes, I did totally see her point.

So, after conducting another interdisciplinary think tank, a physicist came up with the perfect solution: a mini Black Hole to discreetly place inside the trash can. No more need for bags! The waste will just go into the Black Hole, and the integrity of the bin's design can remain untouched.

Vivan was ecstatic. The only drawback is that the Black Hole, mini as it is, does slowly pull everything from the house toward it—but only by a couple of inches a month. It's nothing that can't be managed by pushing back the furniture every now and then. "It's a low price to pay, Julio!" said Vivian. "Thank you once again. I really hated seeing the plastic bags—

I just don't need to see

how the sausage

is made."

Section Three

Gifts That Are Like a Trojan Horse

A gift can help you open hidden doors in your relationship with the receiver. This section will provide gift ideas designed to learn more about the person receiving them, or have them learn more about you. The Statue of Liberty gifts flesh out a relationship you already understand. They expand on an already existing foundation. Trojan Horses are about infiltrating the psyche. They're about discovery. You can also think of them as lanterns guiding you through the crevices of a dark attic (the attic, of course, being the receiver). Common examples of this kind of gift are tarot readings or trips together.

I gave my friends Brandon and Jordan a lamp for their new apartment. I really thought I had nailed it. It's an odd lamp made by an artist I love—the base is a stack of dark burgundy apples, and the shade is like a pleated picnic blanket kind of thing. It sounds odd because it kind of is. I thought it would go great in their place. Unbeknownst to me, I was giving them a Trojan Horse.

I knew this was the case when, after visiting their apartment for the fifth time, I noticed the lamp was still in a corner on the floor. This could mean many things. My lantern is illuminating a shape in the attic, and I'm not sure what that is yet. What I do know is that we love each other, and the fact that they did not display the lamp isn't a manifestation of lack of care, nor is it a little test on my part. But what could it mean? What is this thing I'm seeing in the darkness?

Brandon is brutally honest. If he doesn't like something, he says it. That doesn't rule out that he dislikes the lamp. If that's the case, it says he's protecting me from the truth, that I am spared from his bluntness. Some would say to Brandon, "But I'm your friend, you can be honest!" I say, "Thank God. Keep that thought to yourself." I think he knows this. Our bond is of a different shape than his bond with others.

But then there's the fact the lamp isn't hidden in a closet. It's on the floor. Is this a compromise, or is it unfinished business? It could just mean they're not "little side table" kind of people, that their life together isn't really about "staging" their apartment and having a lamp on the floor is just fine. When I think about it like that, it adds up to how they're a little messy, and how I find that comforting. Maybe what I gave them was evidence that I can be relaxed around them. No coasters, no protocols, no side tables with little lamps on them. That's a friendly figure I'm illuminating in the dark.

A Follow-Up Question

Vivian called. This time she was quite aggravated. I went to her house as soon as I could. Now she was annoyed by elbows. Her own, but also those around her. "They're so wrinkly. I understand that the skin needs to crease on the elbow in order to allow for arms to bend. I get that. I'm not *insane*, but it *is* disgusting; everyone knows that."

"Aha," I said.

"So, perhaps you can talk to some plastic surgeons to get a quote for how much it would cost to smoothen my elbows and the elbows of everyone around me so they're nice and even—"

"Like a Barbie," I interrupted.

Her eyes widened. "Like a *Barbie*. Yes. Very good—make my elbows and the elbows of everyone around me smooth and even, like the skin of a Barbie. Again, I understand why the crease is there; the arm does need to bend, but I just don't need to see how the sausage is made."

At that point I realized I had been doing Vivian a disservice by simply complying with her obsessive little requests. "You keep using that expression. You keep saying, 'I don't need to see how the sausage is made.' What's that about?"

"Well, I . . . I suppose I just don't really need to see how the sausage is made. I don't need to and don't want to see."

"But I guess I wonder why seeing how something functions, or what it takes for a task to happen . . . why is seeing that so upsetting? Like, 'I don't need to see how the sausage is made' uses sausages as the metaphor because I guess the making of a sausage is actually pretty gross, and people don't want to think about that when they're eating them . . ."

"Oh, I sure know the making of sausages is pretty vile, yes. I should know; I'm a Mayer!"

"As in . . . Oscar Mayer Wieners?"

"My great grandfather Oscar, yes."

"So . . . when you say, 'How the sausage is made . . . '"

"The Mayer sausage specifically, yes. My family business. My father always told me not to go into the factory and see how the sausage is made. He always told me to wait in the car whenever he had to stop by late at night for business—business that I was never supposed to tell my mother about. One of those nights, we drove by the factory after getting ice cream and my father said he had to go in for business, which was not unusual. I waited in the car, but then I needed a napkin because my fingers got all sticky from the ice cream—wipe it on my dress and I'd upset my mother, wipe in on the car and I'd upset my father—so I went inside to find something to wipe my hands. I wandered into the dark, empty factory—the smell was putrid. And there, right above the huge industrial meat grinder, I saw my father kissing a young factory worker, in her stained uniform and hairnet. Daddy saw me and got startled. He pushed the woman away; she lost her balance and fell into the meat grinder, which of course then turned her into various sausage links that I suppose got packaged and sold.

"Back in the car, my father was furious. He said to never tell Mommy or anyone. He kept saying, 'I told you to NEVER see how the sausage is made!'"

We sat in silence after her revelation. About a minute later, she stood up and told me to hold off on the elbow thing, that she needed a little time to think. I never heard from her again. This is a good thing. A follow-up question can be a powerful gift.

Little Locked Doors

Not everyone lives an exciting life. Some people work in "offices"; some travel but feel like they've seen it all. We all have a friend like that, a friend who's lost the lust for life.

Boredom comes when you feel like there's nothing more to see . . . but what if a gift can promise excitement, intrigue, a zeal for the unknown? That's what Little Locked Doors are. They're about seven centimeters in height, and come with a little doorknob the receiver can jostle, hoping the door will open, but it won't . . . leaving them to wonder, "What could possibly be behind there?"

Setting these up is easy. Just ask a friend out for lunch and listen to them complain about how dull their life is. Nod along and say, "Perhaps there's still adventure out there . . . perhaps not all doors have been opened." They'll be like, "What?" and you'll smile knowing that while you're at this restaurant, the Little Locked Door is being set up in their cubicle. When they return to their office, they'll find this little riddle, this secret, this question they will never be able to answer. Because these doors can never be opened. That's the point. Every now and then little pieces of mail come, but the letters are addressed to Umberto, so they can't open those, either.

Bloody Knife

Perfect for someone who can't figure out their neighbor. First, the user should sign for a neighbor's package or "accidentally" receive their mail, to lure them in for a quick house visit. Then, the user of the Bloody Knife must set it in an inconspicuous part of their home—on the floor next to a couch, on the floor next to the kitchen counter, or get creative and place it on the floor next to a knocked-over lamp. Basically, the user should stage a little mystery and wait for their neighbor to come get their mail. The real test is the neighbor's reaction to the Bloody Knife. Most will ask something like, "Is everything okay?" Or, "What happened here?" To which the user of the Bloody Knife must reply by saying, "Nothing. It's nothing," and produce a pained smile. Or, preferably, dart their eyes toward a closet, hinting that perhaps something just got out of hand.

Bloody Knife will then showcase what kind of relationship the user has with their neighbor. Best-case scenario, the neighbor nods knowingly and asks no more questions. But if the police get involved, then, well, now the user knows they live next to a snitch who can't keep a secret.

Long Strand of Hair

Sometimes men have a hard time expressing themselves. Sometimes they have a hard time thinking things through. Take my friend's ex (I think his name was Steven?), for example. He would grunt and shake his head as a form of communicating unprocessed thoughts and emotion. That all changed when we gave him a Long Strand of Hair.

Suddenly, Steven could twirl his strand and allow himself to think things through! Emotions were processed, and by the time he got to playing with the end of the strand, he was starting sentences with, "I don't know—I just feel like . . ."

Before that, whenever I saw him he would just sort of look away whenever I spoke, but once he had the Long Strand of Hair, he was able to play with it, focus his attention on it, and say, "I don't know—I just feel like you think I'm some lame guy, so you talk about what *you* want to talk about and don't bother asking me about my day or my life or anything, and then say I have nothing in common with your friend group, which is, like, how would you know?" Fair point, Steven(?)! May you be well, wherever you may be.

Compass to a Secret

Write down a secret, something you've never, ever told anyone, and go as far away as you possibly can. Ideally to a different continent. Bury the piece of paper (or multiple pieces of paper, if it's that juicy) in the secret box and don't tell *anyone* where it is.

Give your friend the Compass, not mentioning anything about the secret. The arrow will point to the box, but it will not say how far away the box is. Should this friend embark on the quest to follow the compass for as long as it takes, the arrow will spin when they finally stand over the box. And your secret will be revealed.

Do make sure you bury that box pretty far away, though. My friend Tabatha wrote down her deepest, darkest secret and buried it just a few miles away. She was ill and the doctors told her she didn't have much time, so she figured the secret wouldn't be unearthed until she was gone, but her friend Janice found it the next day. Now Janice knows Tabatha's kid sister is actually Tabatha's daughter, whom her mother raised as *her* daughter because Tabatha was too young (a classic one of those). I know all this because Janice is a gossip. Tabatha wants her money back, but you *are* supposed to bury the secret very, very far away, so I don't know that she will get a refund.

This gift is for that committed friend who would do anything to know you better.

Tree Bras

You've heard of "tree skirts." They're used by people who have decided their Christmas tree is female and needs to cover up *her* stump. If you know someone like this, it's important to make them examine why they gender and then shame what should be an inanimate, festive object.

The Tree Bra allows you to break the ice in that conversation. When you put the Bra on their tree, chances are this person will find it ridiculous and ask, "What are you doing?" This gives you your in. Respond by saying, "Oh, well, you gave 'her' a skirt. So shouldn't she also have a bra?" To this, expect a puzzled look or a nervous giggle. Keep pressing. "Why should the stump be covered?"

If they just "ha-ha" and move away from you, now you know there's not much between you. If they engage with it, positively or negatively, then you know there's something to discover in the attic of your relationship.

Emotional Tape Measure

It's exactly what it sounds like. A regular tape measure can tell you the physical distance between two points, but an Emotional Tape Measure can show you the *emotional* distance between two *people*.

For example, this couple (person B and person C) are seated at a table together, physically only inches from each other, but an earlier fight about the woman watching the latest episode of *The White Lotus* without the man now has them light years apart.

The woman, B, and a waiter, A, lock eyes while the man, C, mutters rudely about the menu, which is merely an aftershock from the fight earlier over *The White Lotus*. But the waiter has had his share of moody boyfriends, bringing him and the woman emotionally closer, even when he goes several feet away into the kitchen.

The reading of the Emotional Tape Measure changes in real time, taking in the emotional state of both parties almost instantly.

Who is this for? Well, someone who has a hard time reading social cues and would welcome some tangible data regarding how people are feeling about each other.

a.
b.
c.

BAD NEWS BEARS
Deliver the bad news to The Widow
Hit on The Widow
Have another episode
YOU ARE EXPERIENCEING WITHDRAWAL
Get a drink soon

Soldier's Life

A violent video game perfect for kids who enjoy war games.

In *Soldier's Life*, kids aim their virtual gun at enemy soldiers and shoot as many as they can. Once they pass that level, the real game begins: kids must now play from the POVs of the various widows of the soldiers they gunned down, learning their stories, such as what made them happy and their individual family histories, and mourning their husbands.

Does the kid you gave this to end the game once the killing is over? Or do they lean in and learn about those they've gunned down? Do they remember the soldiers' names and think about them once they're done playing, or do they simply move on?

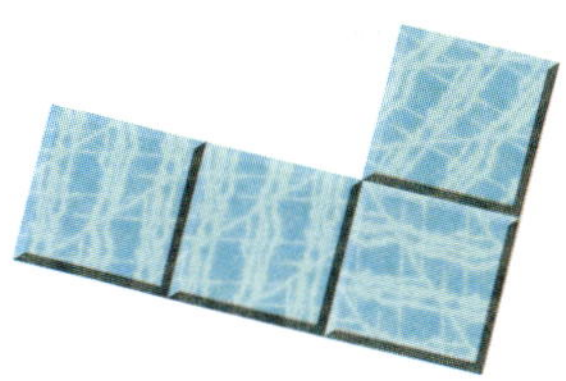

Disintegrating Graph Paper

I've had many frustrating phone conversations with customer support employees. Not because any of them are being difficult or unreasonable, but because their companies are. Whether it's an insurance company that won't cover a prescription it should or an internet provider not providing any indication of when a technician might come, I typically get at least some kind of acknowledgment from the person on the other end of the line that they, somewhere in them, agree that things shouldn't be this way. Sometimes it's a long pause, an "I know," or even an "I am so, so sorry"—a little consolation prize as I concede to losing the battle against their corporate flag.

But there was one time someone not only abided by the senseless rules of their company but also vehemently defended them. I booked a flight to Berlin, and the airline's website asked me to provide my passport information—country of issuance, passport number, etc. As a citizen of El Salvador, I am accustomed to airlines scrutinizing this information, because landing in a country that requires a visa and not having one would be a disaster, and customs blames the airlines. So I booked the flight knowing that I was good to travel to Berlin. Days later, I tell my mother of my travel plans. She asked me where my layover would be. I tell her Toronto.

She then says that I need a visa to get into Canada. "Not for a layover," I tell her. "Are you sure?" she asks. So then I research, and the internet agrees with her, at least at the time. I then call the airline, and they also agree. Securing a Canadian visa takes time I don't have before this trip, plus it's a lot of effort and money to waste on a layover. So I ask to cancel the flight and get a refund. And listen, I know I'm not going to get it, but I'm ready to do the dance. The person on the phone tells me it cannot be done. I ask why. She says it's policy. I say, "Well, the airline, who goes as far as collecting passport information to ensure these kinds of things don't happen, should not have sold me the ticket or should have at least warned me I needed a visa" (like they did for Germany, my final destination). Here, after some back-and-forth, I'm ready to surrender with an "I'm so sorry," "I'll make a note of the incident," or a "Yes, this is very frustrating." Instead, she tells me the airline is correct, because that's the rule.

So it's not even that she disagreed with me; it's that she would not allow herself to think beyond the rule. You can tell me the sky isn't blue if you want to, but at least peek through the window and look at the sky! Not at a piece of paper in front of you describing the sky. I couldn't shake this. I thought about it for days, and that's how I came up with this gift.

I looked her up in the airline directory, found an extension number, inquired about a mailing address, and sent it: a notebook with pages that start out as graph paper but gradually dissolve into senseless lines and eventually completely blank pages. I imagined her receiving it and using it to make lists: grocery lists, to-do lists, budgets, spending logs, all neatly arranged in their cells.

As the pages progressed and the lines disintegrated, I imagined items and numbers turning into sentences. Complete, full sentences at first, mostly about day-to-day life, then eroding further into disembodied thoughts, concepts, ideas, and feelings as those lines got more and more permissive. Then, as the pages began to turn blank—drawings, colors, abstract expressions—and as the notebook came to a close, the pen would wander onto the desk and the office walls, creating graffiti and defacing the invisible graph of the life she lives in.

I came back from Berlin to find the package returned to me. I had written the address wrong. I felt like drawing threes upside down that day. Perhaps what I've illuminated here is not the reason why this person I became so obsessed with is such a stickler for rules. Perhaps what I've only begun to illuminate is my own obstinacy for breaking the norm, even when I don't need to. Perhaps it's connected to how rules have routinely failed me as an immigrant, as the son of someone with crippling debt, or as a citizen of a country where following rules gets you nowhere. That's a scary silhouette I'm illuminating. Turns out I have Trojan Horsed myself.

Eye Contact Latch

A small mirror to be placed over the door latch, at eyeline. It forces you to look into your own eyes as you secure the door at the end of the night, demanding the question: What are you *really* scared of?

Outro

So you've received this book as a gift—what kind of gift is it?

If you've complained about never knowing what to get people, then this guide has been bestowed to you like Prometheus gave fire to humans. Same if you have a wobbly table and someone gave it to you to cushion a short leg.

If you are known to enjoy this type of book, or your friend thinks it will resonate with you or sees you in it, then you've been gifted a Statue of Liberty.

If you have no context for this gift, then you're being investigated. You have been infiltrated. Your reaction will be analyzed. Beware, you have been given a Trojan Horse.

Acknowledgments

Thank you to the many people who made this little gift book possible: Amanda Mulholland, Beth Maglione, Brittany Adames, Cat Boyd, Chris Milea, Hana Park, Ingrid Carabulea, Jamie Selzer, Johanna Li, Jonathan Karp, Kayley Hoffman, Laine Margulies, Laura Wise, Lewelin Polanco, Matthew Monahan, Mindy Marques, Olivia Gerke, Olivia Perrault, Richard Abate.

“I purchased extra copies of this book to keep on hand for when I’m invited to a last-minute party and I need a hostess gift for someone I want to impress. It wouldn’t kill you to do the same.”

—Cole Escola